YA 502.3 S635h
Small, Cathleen,
How to choose your perfect science career /

STEM CAREER CHOICES

How to Choose Your Perfect Science Career

Cathleen Small

CHERITON
CHILDREN'S BOOKS

Published in 2023 by **Cheriton Children's Books**
PO Box 7258, Bridgnorth, Shropshire, WV16 9ET, UK

© 2023 Cheriton Children's Books

First Edition

Author: Cathleen Small
Designer: Paul Myerscough
Editors: Sarah Eason and Jennifer Sanderson
Proofreader: Ella Short

Picture credits: Cover: Shutterstock/Monkey Business Images. Inside: pp. 1, 14, 19: Shutterstock/Rocketclips, Inc.; pp. 1, 24, 29: Shutterstock/VAKS-Stock Agency; p. 4: Shutterstock/Sirichai Saengcharnchai; p. 5: Shutterstock/Studio Romantic; pp. 6, 11, 18: Shutterstock/Monkey Business Images; pp. 6, 22, 28: Shutterstock/Gorodenkoff; pp. 6, 31, 38: Shutterstock/Frame Stock Footage; pp. 7, 41, 48: Shutterstock/GaudiLab; pp. 7, 53: Shutterstock/Microgen; p. 8: Shutterstock/Wavebreakmedia; p. 9: Shutterstock/Lumiereist; pp. 10, 18: Shutterstock/Lordn; p. 12: Shutterstock/Maxbelchenko; pp. 13, 19: Shutterstock/Monkey Business Images; p. 15: Shutterstock/James Kirkikis; p. 16: Shutterstock/Monkey Business Images; p. 17: Shutterstock/Monkey Business Images; pp. 20, 28: Shutterstock/Katy Pack; p. 21: Shutterstock/New Africa; pp. 23, 29: Shutterstock/Keith A Frith; p. 25: Shutterstock/Natascha Kaukorat; p. 26: Shutterstock/Katy Pack; p. 27: Shutterstock/Belushi; p. 30: Shutterstock/Morumotto; pp. 32, 38: Shutterstock/Alpa Prod; p. 33: Shutterstock/Photographee.eu; p. 34: Shutterstock/Robert Kneschke; pp. 35, 39: Shutterstock/Monkey Business Images; p. 36: Shutterstock/Savicic; pp. 37, 39: Shutterstock/Savicic; p. 40: Shutterstock/Naphat Jorjee; pp. 42, 48: Shutterstock/MDV Edwards; p. 43: Shutterstock/Viktoriia Hnatiuk; pp. 44, 49: Shutterstock/Jacob Lund; pp. 45, 49: Shutterstock/Spotmatik Ltd; p. 46: Shutterstock/GaudiLab; p. 47: Shutterstock/GaudiLab; pp. 50, 58: Shutterstock/Gorodenkoff; pp. 51, 58: Shutterstock/R Classen; pp. 52, 59: Shutterstock/Couperfield; pp. 54, 59: Shutterstock/Cast Of Thousands; p. 56: Shutterstock/Alexandru-Radu Borzea; p. 57: Shutterstock/Sandra Matic; p. 60: Shutterstock/Monkey Business Images; p. 61: Shutterstock/Cookie Studio.

All rights reserved. No part of this book may be reproduced in any form without permission from the publisher, except by a reviewer.

Printed in China

Please visit our website,
www.cheritonchildrensbooks.com
to see more of our high-quality books.

CONTENTS

CHAPTER ONE
WHO DO YOU THINK YOU ARE?................4

CHAPTER TWO
HELPER ROLES IN SCIENCE...................10

CHAPTER THREE
BUILDER ROLES IN SCIENCE..................20

CHAPTER FOUR
CREATOR ROLES IN SCIENCE.................30

CHAPTER FIVE
ORGANIZER ROLES IN SCIENCE..............40

CHAPTER SIX
THINKER ROLES IN SCIENCE..................50

WHAT NEXT?—YOUR CAREER CHECKLIST......60

GLOSSARY....................................62
FIND OUT MORE............................63
INDEX AND ABOUT THE AUTHOR............64

CHAPTER ONE
WHO DO YOU THINK YOU ARE?

If you're interested in a career in science, there are many different paths to choose from. So how do you discover which career is the right one for you? This book will help you narrow down the choices and find a path that suits you.

Finding Your Place

Science is a constantly changing and developing field with many different exciting career paths that you can follow. Do you have an idea of what you want to do in the world of science? You might, but if not, don't worry—there is plenty of time to figure out exactly what you want to do. This book will help you take the first step in deciding what to do next. It will also help you start to define your interests in the larger field of science and narrow down options.

The world of science is part of almost every area of our modern lives, from our healthcare systems to how we source and utilize the energy that we need. And science careers feature in all of these areas. With so many available choices, how do you start narrowing down your search for a career in science? One way to begin is by identifying your personality type and then looking at the types of careers that are often a good fit for people who share the same personality type as you. So let's get started!

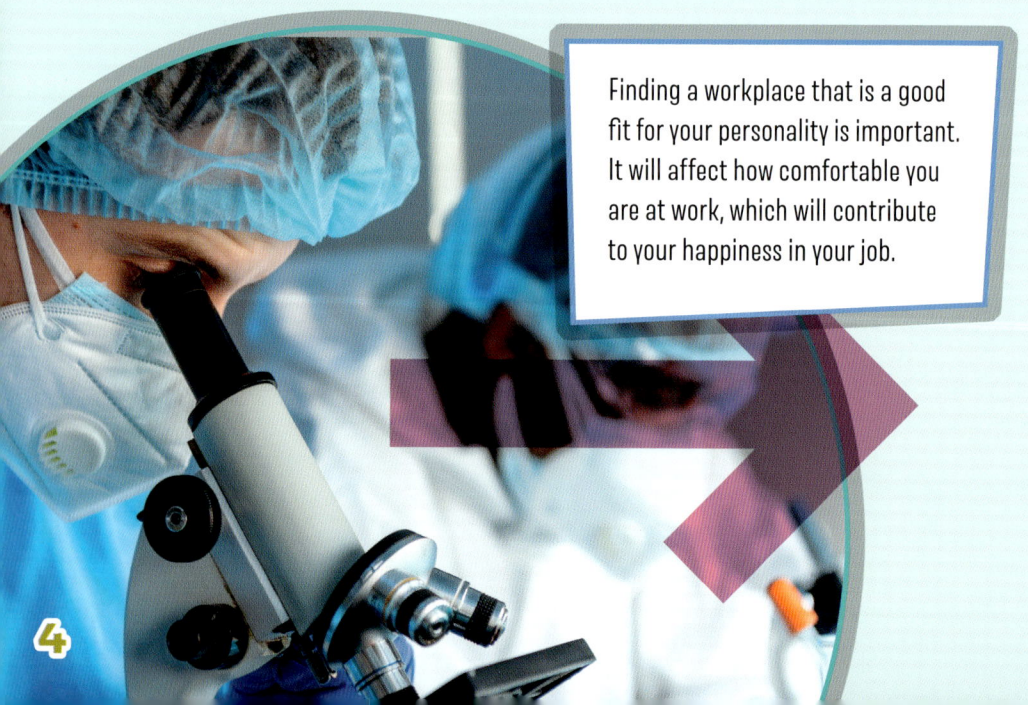

Finding a workplace that is a good fit for your personality is important. It will affect how comfortable you are at work, which will contribute to your happiness in your job.

It can take a while to find a career that suits you, but it's important not to rush decisions and to take your time. Your long-term goal is to find a role in science in which you are fulfilled and happy.

Follow the Flowchart to Fast-Track Your Future!

To find your personality type, you'll need to work through the flowchart on the following pages. The flowchart asks you simple questions to help you determine your personality type. This is based on five types of personality and the work situations that typically appeal to people with those types of personality. The five personality types in the flowchart are: social; practical; creative; organized; and analytical.

These personality types correspond to five different work environments. Social people, for example, often enjoy helper types of careers. Practical people often thrive in builder types of jobs. Creative people flourish in creator roles. Organized people typically enjoy organizational roles. And analytical people usually gravitate to thinking jobs. Although flowcharts are not foolproof, the one in this book should help steer you in the right direction.

Exploring your personality type and career options is important because if you work in an area that is a good fit for you, you will be more likely to be satisfied and successful. And that, in turn, will lead to greater overall happiness with your life. So take a look at the flowchart on the next pages and work through it to determine your career personality type. Then, follow the next steps to find your perfect career in science.

This flowchart asks you questions about your preferences to help you figure out which of the five personality types best describes you. It helps you think about what you like and don't like, and what kind of work might be best for you, so you can make sound career choices.

Once you have figured out what your career type is, take a look at the career choices in this book. Each chapter features some interesting careers linked to the personality types shown in the flowchart on these pages. A variety of jobs are explored in each chapter, along with a day in the life of one of the roles featured. Each chapter concludes with a checklist that helps you work through how you feel about the featured jobs and if they may be right for you.

Helper

Are you interested in helping people and the environment?

No, this is not an area I want to work in

Yes, I want to make a positive contribution to people's lives and the environment

Do you like working in a practical, hands-on way?

No, I hate having to be practical

Yup, I am super practical

Builder

WHAT'S YOUR CAREER TYPE?

Creator

Organizer

Thinker

Are you artistic or creative?
- That's me! → Creator
- No, art's not my thing! → Do you love having things in order?

Do you love having things in order?
- Yes! Check that box! → Organizer
- No, I don't care about that → Do you enjoy studying and thinking through complex ideas?

Do you enjoy studying and thinking through complex ideas?
- Yes, I love theories and thinking through ideas → Thinker
- No, I don't enjoy complicated study → If you have made it all the way to this box, try taking the test again—you can work through it a few times before you finalize your answer.

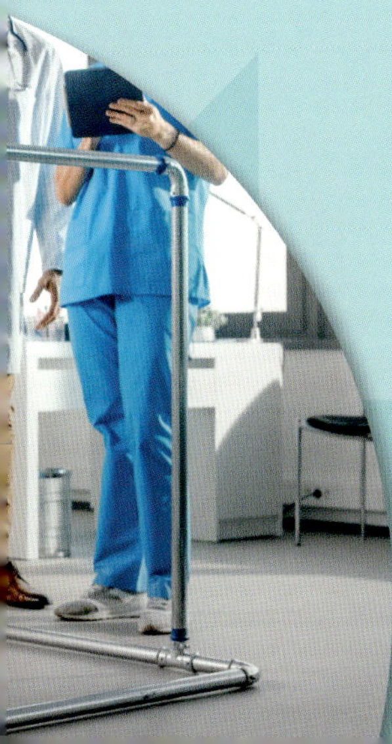

At this stage of your life, you have time to figure out what you want to do in the future. Invest in plenty of research and think through each option to make sure it feels right for your personality type.

What Did You Learn?

Did you discover anything new about yourself from the flowchart? Did you find your perfect career personality? Maybe there was one that fitted you like a glove, and you're ready to explore that particular type of science career. But not so fast! Did any others fit you, too? Maybe not quite as well, but still a possible fit? If so, you'll want to explore that part of the book, too. Remember, flowcharts aren't flawless, and your perfect science career might be lurking in an unexpected place.

It's not unusual to be unsure of exactly which work personality type is your exact fit. Many people find they're a combination of more than one. For example, many analytical people also have a creative side. You don't have to be just one type.

Weed Out the Nos

Even if you didn't find a perfect match for your career personality, you probably found some personality types that definitely do not fit you. If you're not at all organized, for example, you can probably rule out career paths that typically appeal to organized people.

If you feel a little unsure about your career personality type from the flowchart, try again and don't force yourself to fit just one type. Weed out the definite nos, and then review the remaining career personality types and try to determine which ones might be the closest fit.

What to Do with the Yesses

Once you've identified your best fits, work through this book to learn more about the career areas that are best suited to your personality type or types. Each chapter covers specific science careers that often are a good fit for the given personality type.

Start with the chapters for the career personality types that seem a best fit but don't miss the other chapters, too. You never know what career might resonate with you, even if at first that career personality type doesn't seem like a close match.

Explore Options

This book covers many options in the field of science but not all of them. You can read the book to get started and then explore further. The Review and Check In sections at the end of each chapter feature further career options you could research. And once you reach the end of the book, the What Next? checklist will guide you through taking the next steps to kick-start your career.

Career Insight: Nothing Is Ever Set in Stone

Always remember that nothing is ever permanent. If you enter a career and find you do not enjoy it, it is not the end of the world. You can certainly switch to another career in the field or even switch to an entirely different field. The important thing is to keep checking in with yourself and make sure you are on a path that feels right for you.

Take every opportunity to find out about different courses in the science career areas that you are interested in.

CHAPTER TWO
HELPER ROLES IN SCIENCE

If you're a person who likes to help people or animals, the science world has many career options for you to choose from. Doctors, researchers, nurses, medical assistants, and radiologists, veterinarians and veterinary technicians are part of the science field, and they are all helpers in their own way.

Doctor

One of the most obvious helper jobs in the field of science is a doctor. Doctors help people by diagnosing and treating people's illnesses and injuries. Doctors need to be able to see the bigger picture to figure out what is wrong with a person. They also need to be empathetic so that the patient feels comfortable telling them about their ailments.

To become a doctor takes dedication and hard work, especially if you want to specialize in a specific field. To begin your medical career, you'll need to earn a bachelor's degree from a college or university that is accredited by medical school admissions boards. Following your degree, you must pass the Medical College Admission Test (MCAT), which is a test to assess a candidate's

There are many years of training ahead if you want to become a doctor but the rewards of the job long-term are great.

> Nurses provide invaluable care and support to people who need healthcare. It is a truly hands-on role that brings great job satisfaction to people who enjoy science and helping others.

likelihood of succeeding at medical school. When you've passed this, you can apply to a medical school. Medical school lasts four years but to practice medicine, you'll need to pass the first and second parts of the United States Medical Licensing Examination (USMLE). After that, you'll begin a residency, which can last seven years, depending on the area of medicine you want to specialize in. The final step in the residency process is to complete part three of the USMLE. Once you've done this, you can earn board certifications for your specialized field. Trained and board-certified doctors must then apply for a state license before they enter the field.

Nurse

While doctors often get a lot of the attention in the medical world, the role of a nurse is not to be underestimated. Nurses are incredibly valuable in on-the-ground patient care and often, a nurse will see the patient for much longer than the doctor does. A nurse is usually the first person a patient will see, and if a patient is in distress, the nurse is often the one to respond to the crisis.

Nurses can follow several educational paths to reach their goal. To become a registered nurse (RN), you can earn a four-year Bachelor of Science in nursing (BSN) degree. You can also complete a two-year associate's degree in nursing or a diploma from an approved nursing program; however, it may be more difficult to find a job, and the pay may not be as high. Some employers insist that their registered nurses have the BSN degree. On any of these three paths, you must pass a state licensing exam to become a registered nurse.

Over the last few years, all healthcare professionals, including nurses and orderlies, have been responsible for trying to limit infectious disease in healthcare settings due to the Covid-19 pandemic.

Nursing Assistant

If a college degree is not for you but you would like to pursue a career in nursing, you could consider being a nursing assistant. Nursing assistants provide basic patient care either in a hospital setting or in a rehabilitation or nursing home. Being a nursing assistant is a good way to see if you enjoy nursing before spending time and money studying for a nursing degree. To be a nursing assistant, you'll need a high school diploma and must complete a state-approved training program that is usually offered through a community college or vocational school. Each state has a competency exam that nursing assistants must pass before they can enter the field.

Orderly

An orderly is a trained healthcare professional who works in a hospital or medical practice under the direct supervision of the nursing staff. Orderlies provide care and comfort to patients. Some of their duties include helping patients to dress and bathe and transporting patients from their beds to different departments for tests and procedures. In a hospital, orderlies may also need to perform routine cleaning or disinfecting to help prevent the spread of disease or infection.

To be an orderly requires a high school diploma and you'll need on-the-job training. Like nursing assistants, orderlies have to pass a competency exam for their state before they can practice.

If you enjoy working with people and helping others, and have an interest in healthcare, being an orderly could be a good career.

Career Insight:
Not Just in Hospitals

Most nurses work either in hospitals or in doctor's offices but that's not true for all nurses, for example, many schools have their own nurse, too. There are other nursing jobs you might not have thought of, too. For example, camp nurses: The majority of camps have a nurse on staff, in case any campers are injured. This includes camps for children with illnesses or disabilities as well as standard summer camps and high-adventure camps. Tourist attractions such as Disneyland and Disney World have nurses on staff for the same reason.

Another interesting nursing field is sports and activities. For example, NASCAR auto racing has nurses on staff to administer care when drivers are injured or to monitor drivers who are recovering from a past injury or illness. Flight nurses accompany patients who are being transported by helicopter or airplane. Most often, these are critical-care patients, so the nurses who work with them need to be exceptionally skilled in trauma care and life support.

And finally, Hollywood is forever producing television shows and movies about the medical field, and they often consult with medical professionals so that their shows will be as realistic as possible. This isn't usually a full-time position but it can be an interesting job to do on the side.

Caring for people's pets as a vet is a responsible job. You need to be sympathetic to owners' feelings while applying your scientific skills to animal care.

Doctor of Veterinary Medicine

If you like to help others and you really love animals, you might want to consider a science career working with animals, and at the top of the list is a doctor of veterinary medicine (DVM), better known as a vet.

To be a vet, you'll need to work hard and study for several years. First you'll need to go to college to earn a bachelor's degree and then, you'll need to apply for vet school. Vet school takes four years to complete. Once you've completed vet school, you'll need to pass a licensing exam before you can practice. Depending on the state you're practicing in, you may need to pass a state exam in addition to the national exam.

Vet school is highly competitive, and there are only 32 accredited veterinary medicine programs in the United States that take a limited number of candidates. So, if you're interested in becoming a vet, be sure to make yourself look like a top-notch applicant: Take a lot of science classes, especially in the life sciences, and make sure your bachelor's degree is in a relevant field.

Vet Technician and Assistant

If you like working with animals but you don't want to invest the time and money in pursuing a full DVM degree, you might want to consider a career as a veterinary technician or a veterinary assistant. Vet techs administer anesthetic during surgical procedures, take X-rays and blood, administer vaccines, and prepare animals for surgery. There are two-year and four-year programs for those who want to become veterinary technicians, and they must pass a credentialing exam before they can begin work as a technician.

Veterinary assistants typically don't need any education beyond a high school diploma. Some even begin working part-time as veterinary assistants while in high school—this is a great way to get valuable experience if you're interested in becoming a vet. The job usually involves feeding, bathing, and exercising animals, keeping their cages clean, and caring for them after surgical procedures.

Career Insight:
Other Jobs with Animals

If you're interested in a science career working with animals but want to do more than work with pets, there are other options. Some veterinarians work specifically at zoos with many different types of animal.

If you'd rather work with animals out in the wild, you might want to consider being a zoologist or a wildlife biologist. Though they can work in zoos, they often work out in the field, with animals in their natural habitats. You could also be a wildlife rehabilitator. Often these professionals work at wildlife hospitals or rehabilitation centers. They work with wild animals that are sick or that have been injured—usually with the goal of trying to reintroduce the animal into the wild.

Working in a zoo can be a great career for people who enjoy caring for animals and carrying out scientific research too.

A DAY IN THE LIFE OF
A Hospital Nurse

There's no doubt that nursing is a fast-paced, demanding job, but it's also a very rewarding one. You get to work hands-on with patients and no two days are the same.

5:00 a.m. This week you're on the day shift, so you need to be at work at 7:00 a.m. sharp to relieve the night shift nurses. The day shift is always a lot busier than night shift but you'd rather be busy and you prefer daytime work.

7:00 a.m. You meet with nurses on the night shift to get patient updates and any other information you need to be aware of. You review patient charts and physician notes to familiarize yourself with them before you start your rounds.

8:00 a.m. You check in with each patient and do bloodwork or other tests that the physician requested. You also need to administer any medications. Most patients need help with daily activities, such as eating, so you ask one of the nursing assistants to help you with this. These morning rounds take several hours, because each nurse is assigned to many patients. There's rarely a dull moment in the hospital.

> Keeping patients calm and happy is an essential part of nursing. Patients look to you for reassurance and comfort.

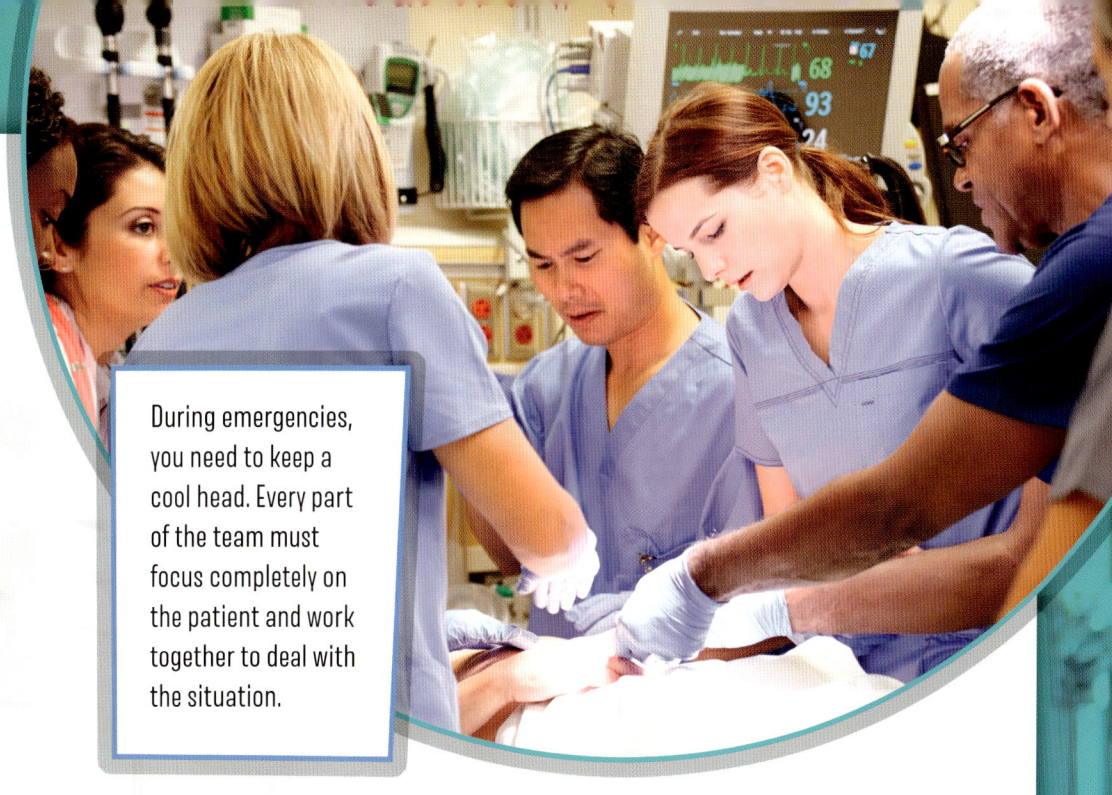

During emergencies, you need to keep a cool head. Every part of the team must focus completely on the patient and work together to deal with the situation.

12:00 a.m. You spend a few minutes off your feet at the nurses' station. By law, every employee must have a break but in a busy hospital, if an emergency arises, you may find your break delayed.

1:00 p.m. It's time to begin afternoon rounds. Like morning rounds, afternoon rounds take several hours. There are a lot of patients who need attention. You check that all your patients needing medication get their correct dose and you order a blood test for a new patient who has just arrived on your ward. You make sure the patient is settled before moving onto the next one. There's a young boy who had his appendix out and is ready to be discharged, so you go through his homecare instructions with his parents. You need to check that the boy will have adequate supervision and care at home.

5:00 p.m. You need to catch up on your charting so you can brief the night shift when they arrive for their 7:00 shift. Just as you're getting into a good rhythm, one of your patients rings his bell. You go over to his bed to check on him. He feels hot and is sweaty so you take his vitals. He may have an infection setting in, so you call the doctor to assess him.

6:00 p.m. The night shift nurses have arrived, so you brief them on anything they'll need to know to care for the patients overnight. You're worried about the patient with the infection, so you ask your friend on the night shift to keep a close eye on him to make sure he is stable.

7:00 p.m. Your shift is done and the night nurses are ready, so you go home to get an early night. It's been a long day.

Helper
Review and Check In

Now that you've learned about some of the helper roles in science, explore more about how you feel about each job. Use the questions below to help you assess how strongly you feel each role might suit you.

Doctor
- Are you happy and motivated to pursue the further education required to be a doctor?
- What makes you well-suited to this career?
- Being a doctor can be stressful. How would you deal with the stress that comes with the job?
- When you consider the lifestyle you would like in the future, does this job suit it? Why or why not?

Nurse
- Often nurses do jobs that many people wouldn't like to do. What parts of the job would you find challenging and how could you deal with them?
- What personality traits would help you be a good nurse? Are there things you could improve on?

Nursing Assistant
- Would you be able to work in a team of assistants and nurses? What skills do you have to enable this?
- What part of this job would be the most rewarding? What would be the least?

"Always keep in mind what you want from your career."

"Make sure you choose a job that motivates you—one that makes you want to get up every day and go to work."

Orderly
- You need to be able to follow instructions to be an orderly. Would that suit you? Why?
- What skills do you have that you think could fit the role?

Vet Technician and Assistant
- Why would you like to be a vet technician or assistant?
- What skills do you have that would make you a good vet technician or assistant?
- What challenges do you think you might encounter in this role?
- Would you be able to work in a team, taking instruction from vets? Why do you say so?

Vet
- Are you willing to work extremely hard to get into vet school? What can you do to ensure your application stands out?
- Being a vet is one of the most stressful jobs. Why do you think this is so? How would you deal with those stresses?

"Always think, 'What am I good at?' then find a career that suits your skills."

Research More

If you like the idea of working as a helper in science, but are not sure the jobs covered in this chapter suit you, here are some more helper roles you could explore.

Conservation Scientist and Forester
Soil and Plant Scientist
Pollution and Prevention Control Officer

CHAPTER THREE
BUILDER ROLES IN SCIENCE

If you like to be hands-on in whatever you're doing, actively constructing solutions, you probably scored high on the builder roles. While many science fields involve analysis and thinking more than building, there are also jobs in science for builders, from building prosthetic devices for people who have lost limbs and new organs and tissues for patients to building clean energy solutions.

Prosthetist and Orthotist

While doctors and therapists work with patients who have lost limbs in accidents or as a result of injury or illness, there are medical professionals who build the artificial limbs that some of these patients receive. They are called prosthetists. Prosthetists must determine which type of prosthetic will best serve their patient.

A closely related field to prosthetics is orthotics. Orthotics are artificial supports for limbs or the spine. People may require orthotics if they have an injured limb that still exists but that isn't working quite right. For example, many people with foot problems wear orthotics in their shoes. People who build and fit orthotic devices are called orthotists.

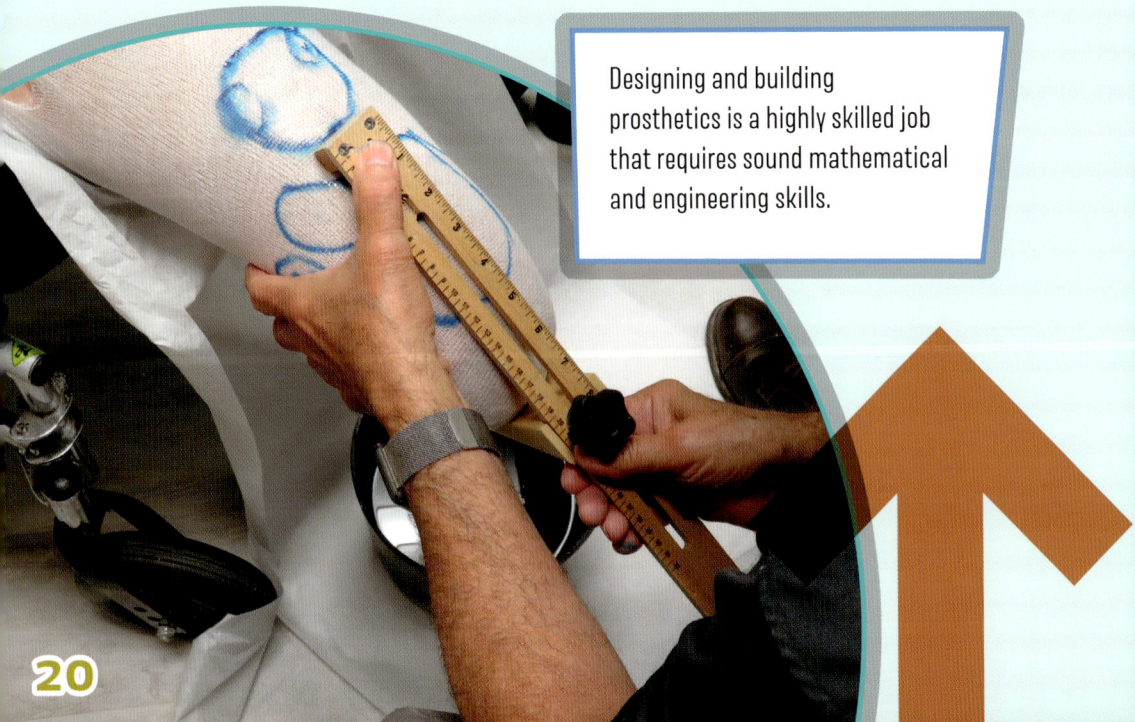

Designing and building prosthetics is a highly skilled job that requires sound mathematical and engineering skills.

Orthotists and prosthetists work closely with their patients to educate them about the devices they will be using and how best to use and maintain them.

Although premade orthotic inserts for shoes and generic splints and braces can be bought in stores, in the case of serious injury, orthotics are custom-made for each patient. To make sure these are exactly correct, orthotists work with patients to determine their needs, including taking careful measurements, because orthotic devices are generally custom-made for each patient. Many orthotists and prosthetists then fashion the orthotic or prosthetic device themselves and fit it to the patient. They also instruct the patient in how to care for and maintain the device.

If you're interested in a career as an orthotist or prosthetist, you'll need a bachelor's degree (preferably in a science field) and master's degree in orthotics and prosthetics. There is usually a clinical requirement, too, where students work under the supervision of an experienced orthotist or prosthetist. In addition, after graduating from the master's program, orthotists and prosthetists must completed a one-year residency in either field. Depending on the state, they may also need to pass a certification exam to practice.

Medical Appliance Technician

Although prosthetists and orthotists can build their own devices, sometimes they delegate the actual designing and building of prosthetics and orthotics to a medical appliance technician. Medical appliance technicians can also make other devices, including eye glasses and dental devices. To be a medical appliance technician, you'll need a high school diploma or GED. Usually technicians don't have to have any further schooling beyond that. They learn their trade on the job.

Robotics is a fascinating area of biomedical engineering. This exoskeleton, or robotic suit, has been developed to assist people who have difficulties walking.

Biomedical Engineer

If you're interested in building new tissues or organs, biomedical engineering is a field that might interest you. Biomedical engineering advancements have now become part of standard patient care—for example, there are mechanical heart valves used in some patients, and patients can be fitted with artificial hip and knee joints—and play an important role in saving lives and helping people to live more comfortably. Biomedical engineers not only design such devices, they also maintain and repair the devices as needed.

For those interested in becoming a biomedical engineer, a bachelor's degree in biomedical engineering or bioengineering is a good place to start. However, some biomedical engineers have begun their careers with a bachelor's degree in a more general field of engineering, such as mechanical or electrical engineering. Electrical engineering might sound a little odd but the body's nervous system essentially works on electrical impulses, so it's more related than you might think. Sometimes, the devices are electrical too—for example, the incredibly successful pacemaker, which has saved the lives of millions of people worldwide by regulating heart rates, is an electrical device.

Environmental Engineer

If you're more interested in environmental science than in working with human patients or devices for people, you might be interested in working as an environmental engineer.

Career Insight: Genetic Engineering

If you like to build but are interested in building on the most microscopic levels, you could think about a career in genetic engineering or genetic modification. Genetic engineers take apart and rebuild the genetic codes of organisms from viruses to sheep and humans. For example, genetic engineering can be used to produce plants with a high nutritional value or it can be used to find cures for diseases and conditions that have plagued humans or animals for countless generations. It's microscopic, precise work—building at its very tiniest, most basic level.

Environmental engineers have a strong knowledge of earth science, biology, chemistry, and engineering, and build solutions to environmental problems. For example, they may develop recycling and waste disposal solutions, water-storage solutions, and alternative energy solutions. Their work involves on-site investigations as well as sitting at a desk, so this is a good career choice if you don't like to be office-bound.

Environmental engineers usually have a bachelor's degree in environmental engineering or a related engineering field. Other options include civil and chemical engineering. A bachelor's degree is usually enough for an entry-level environmental engineering position, but if you're interested in doing research or management, you'll need to earn a master's degree too.

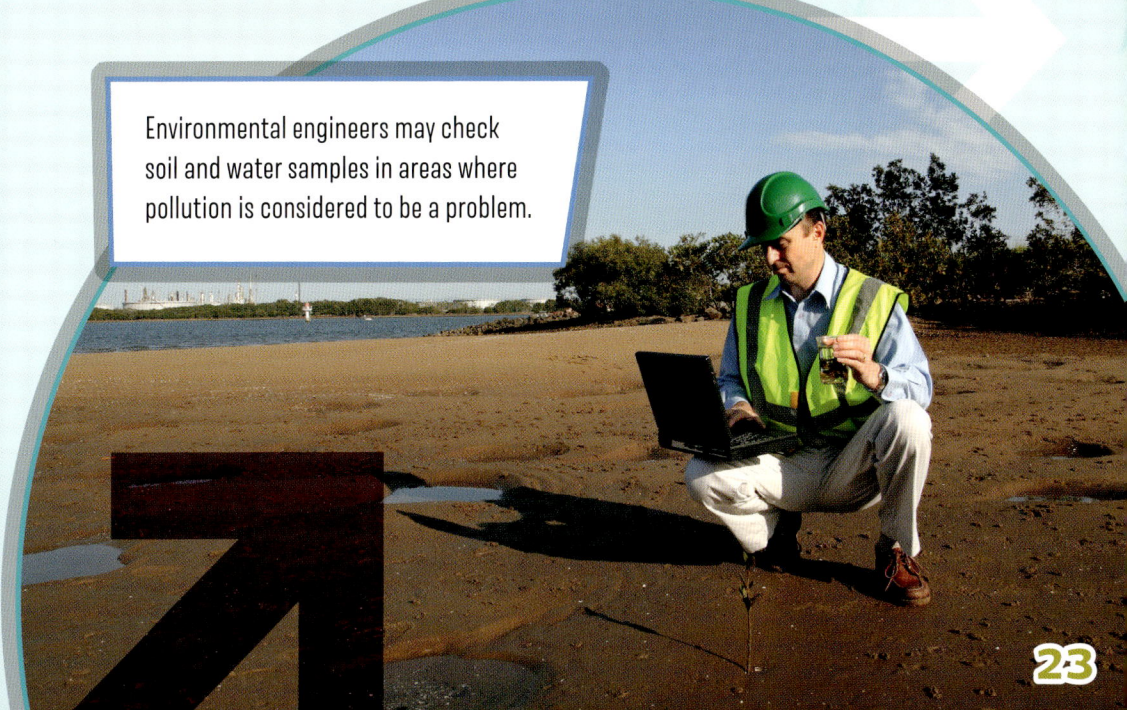

Environmental engineers may check soil and water samples in areas where pollution is considered to be a problem.

Installing renewable energy technology is a rapidly growing job field and one that has great future potential. This engineer is installing a solar panel.

Alternative Energy Installer and Technician

If further studying is not for you and you'd prefer a career where you can start earning a living straight out of school while you train on the job, you might want to consider a career in installing or maintaining environmental solutions. Environmental solutions include alternative energy solutions as well as waste and recycling solutions.

As the world moves toward cleaner energy solutions, one rapidly growing field is solar energy. Many businesses and homeowners are installing solar photovoltaics to use the sun's energy to produce electricity rather than unclean energy sources. Solar photovoltaic installers put together solar panels and install and maintain them on roofs or other structures. In sunny places where there is a lot of open space, solar farms can be built—these have thousands of photovoltaic panels and they all need maintaining and servicing.

Solar photovoltaic installers must have a high school diploma. Some learn the trade on the job, and others take classes at a vocational school or community college before getting into the field and beginning work.

Solar isn't the only alternative power source. Wind power is becoming more widely used, too. Although some people install small wind turbines at their home to capture wind energy and convert it into power for their home, more commonly you'll see vast fields or hillsides dotted with large wind turbines, all working to capture the wind's energy as a clean power source. Someone has to install and maintain those wind turbines and those people are highly skilled wind turbine technicians.

Wind turbine technicians typically have a high school degree but they also attend technical school or community college to earn a certificate in wind energy technology. This coursework not only teaches them about wind power technology and the specific systems used but it also gives them safety training. Wind turbines are very tall, so there is a danger involved in working on them. Technicians need to be trained and certified in safety and first aid. In addition to schooling, wind turbine technicians generally receive on-the-job training specific to the types of turbines they'll be servicing.

Today, many farmers are devoting areas of their farmland to growing crops for biofuel, such as this rapeseed crop.

Career Insight:
Back to the Farm

In the past, farming and agriculture were thriving careers in the United States. In recent years, though, farms have dwindled. Today, as a result of the focus on alternative energy, farming is once again becoming a good career possibility. Instead of growing food crops for consumption, many farmers are now growing food to be used as bioenergy. Corn, for example, can be used to fuel cars, and soybean, wheat, coconut, and sugar cane farmers can contribute to the biofuel and biodiesel markets.

A DAY IN THE LIFE OF
A Prosthetist

Every day looks different when you're a prosthetist and no two patients have the same needs but this should give you an idea of an average day.

8:00 a.m. You like to arrive at least 30 minutes before you have to see patients. This gives you time to check your emails and messages to see whether anything needs immediate attention. You also need to check in with your office staff to see whether any urgent calls have come in from the hospital—hospital emergencies mean you need to alter your schedule. It's been a good night—there are no emergencies so far!

8:30 a.m. Your first patient of the day is an amputee who lost his leg in a motorcycle accident. He has now healed enough after surgery to be a good candidate for a prosthetic leg. You examine his leg, interview him, and take extensive measurements for the prosthetic. You don't like to build the prosthetics yourself, so you'll pass on all this information to the lab that is making the limb.

9:30 a.m. The second patient of the day is a young woman who was born without her left arm. She has spent most of her life adapting and just using her right arm but now she wants to try a prosthetic. You took her measurements several weeks ago and her prosthetic arm is finished and ready to be fitted. The patient is emotional and excited about this new stage in her life so you carefully fit the arm and adjust it for comfort. You spend time teaching her to use it but you also comfort her as she experiences a lot of emotions. She's spent her whole life with only one arm, and it's a big adjustment for her to have two.

> You always try to show care and compassion when working with your patients. Many have been traumatized by their limb loss.

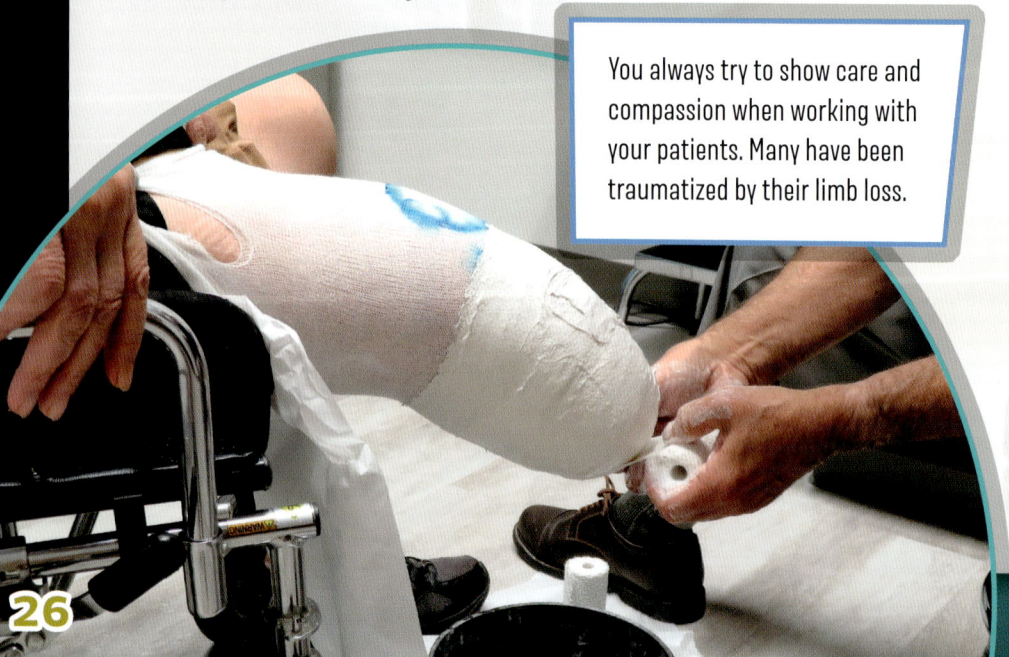

Sometimes, you have to refine the prosthetic and then refit it when it has been improved.

11:00 a.m. When your patient leaves, you sit at your desk and write notes on her session. These will help you when you see her again for a check up. You take a quick call from a colleague who is interested in hearing about a new type of prosthetic hand you used on a patient a few weeks ago. It's groundbreaking, and you're excited to share your experience.

11:30 a.m. It's early but you have a busy afternoon so you quickly head out to get some lunch. It will be your last chance to eat.

11:45 a.m. A call comes in from the hospital. They have an emergency case that they need a consultation on right away. You ask your office staff to push back your appointments while you head over to the hospital to examine the arm of a patient who was in a bad car accident. You and the emergency room (ER) doctor confer and decide that the patient's arm cannot be saved but that he is a good candidate for a prosthetic arm in the future.

1:30 p.m. You're back in the office, ready to see patients again. Fortunately, they understand that emergencies have to take priority.

4:00 p.m. Your final patient of the day, a child who needs a prosthetic leg, is a troubling one. The leg that the lab made does not fit perfectly and is causing the child pain. You tell the disappointed child and his parents that you'll have to start over and have the lab create a new leg—none of the adjustments you've made to the one they sent have made it comfortable for the child. You set about taking all new measurements to try again.

5:30 p.m. You finally leave the office and head home. It's been a good day, but tiring!

Builder
Review and Check In

Now that you've learned about some of the builder roles in science, explore more about how you feel about each job. Use the questions below to help you assess how strongly you feel each role might suit you.

Prosthetist and Orthotist
- Trying to help a person to make their daily life easier can be very rewarding. What else about this work would you find satisfying?
- What do you think you would find most challenging about being an orthotist or a prosthetist? How would you deal with those challenges?

Biomedical Engineer
- What attracts you to studying to be a biomedical engineer?
- What skills do you have that you think could fit the role? What skills do you think you would need to work on?

Medical Appliance Technician
- What aspects of the job do you think you would enjoy? Are there aspects that you don't think you'll enjoy? Why do you say so?
- What field interests you the most? Are you prepared to study further to specialize in this field?

"When choosing a career, always consider the career outlook—does your chosen area have potential in the future?"

"Think about the training involved in the career you are interested in. Are you happy to undertake it?"

Alternative Energy Installer and Technician
- Most of your day would be spent outdoors doing manual work. Why would this suit your personality and skills set?
- You could choose to work for yourself or for a larger firm. What are the pros and cons of each one?

Environmental Engineer
- Why do you want to make a difference by working in this role?
- What field of environmental engineering interests you most? Why?
- Are you an innovative problem solver? What other skills do you have that would suit this job?
- Is there anything that you do not like about the role? What is that? Do the benefits of the job outweigh the aspects you may not like?

"Think about what your work environment might be like. Would it suit you? Would you be happy there?"

Research More

If you like the idea of working as a builder in science, but are not sure the jobs covered in this chapter suit you, here are some more builder roles you could explore.

Nuclear Technician
Space Scientist
Oceanographer

CHAPTER FOUR
CREATOR ROLES IN SCIENCE

You might wonder how many jobs in the field of science there are for a creative person. After all, people have long thought that logical, analytical people are more left-brained, while creative, artistic people are right-brained. It is true that the left and right halves, or hemispheres, of the brain process tasks differently but it is not true that people use either their left brain or their right brain more. People use both sides of their brain, and there's no evidence that people use one side any more than the other. So, the creative people among us can have just as much skill in logical areas, like science, as anyone else. And there are many careers that allow them to use their creative talents while working in the field of science.

Multimedia Artist and Animator

In the movie, television, and gaming industries, animation, effects, and graphics play a big part. Multimedia artists and animators typically use software to create two- and three-dimensional (2-D and 3-D) models, graphics, and visual effects for use in movies, television, gaming, and other media. Some start by drawing out their ideas the old-fashioned way but then transfer the images into software programs. Other animators like to start right in the program.

You'll likely recognize this animation from the movie *Finding Dory*! The character was originated by artists at Pixar Animation Studios.

30

Working as part of a team of animators allows you to brainstorm ideas. Collaborating in this way can be enjoyable and usually results in an improved end product.

Multimedia artists and animators generally work in teams—it takes far more than one person to animate a complex project like a movie or television episode. Even for games, effects and animation are typically a team effort. However, it is possible to work independently building your own app with graphics and animation, but it's not common to do so. As well as having the right credentials, you'll need to be a team player and someone who gets on well with other people.

To become a multimedia artist or animator, you'll need a bachelor's degree in computer graphics, fine art, animation, or a related field. You'll also need a portfolio of your work, which you can start developing immediately. Your portfolio is an always-changing collection of your best work. As you add new pieces to it, you might take out some older pieces that you no longer think represent your best work.

If you are an enormously talented artist with a standout portfolio and computer skills in digital art software, you might be able to get a job just based on your talent. However, you'll have many more opportunities if you have a bachelor's degree. The bachelor's degree will ensure that you have a good, well-rounded set of artistic skills and knowledge that will make you a good candidate for jobs.

Career Insight:
Solving Through Animation

One great way to combine an interest in science with a talent for art is to be a forensic animator. Forensic animators work with the police force, detectives, lawyers, and witnesses to create reenactments of the crime. These reenactments can help investigation teams solve crimes and can be used in court to show a jury what the police believe happened during a crime. Another interesting way to combine artistic talent with science is to be a medical illustrator or animator. These skilled professionals create 2-D and 3-D representations of body systems that can be used as learning tools for medical professionals.

Occupational Therapist and Physical Therapist

Occupational therapy and physiotherapy blend science and medical knowledge with creativity. Occupational therapy focuses on helping people develop skills needed for daily living, which may be delayed or lost because of certain health conditions, illnesses, or injuries. Physical therapy focuses on helping people improve movement and manage pain, often as the result of injury or illness they have suffered.

Helping people learn to walk again after injury or illness requires great patience and empathy for patients. It also demands a sound understanding of the mechanics of the human body.

Occupational therapy generally works on fine-motor skills, which involve using small muscles to perform precise activities. For example, writing with a pen or pencil uses the small muscles of the hand to produce very precise movements. For people struggling with handwriting, occupational therapists can help them build up the strength of their hand muscles to write. Physical therapy generally works on gross-motor skills, which involve larger muscles in the arms, legs, and torso. Gross-motor skills include walking, running, hopping, throwing, and so on.

Both physical and occupational therapists have to be creative when working with patients. Their patients may be young children with developmental delays, who often have short attention spans and don't really want to work on things such as handwriting or learning how to hop.

Their patients may also be older people who are recovering from surgery or an injury that has caused a lot of pain. Those patients may be frustrated and not very eager to experience more pain as they learn to walk again.

To get their patients to be willing to do the hard work, therapists have to come up with innovative ways to inspire them. For example, young children may not want to work on handwriting but many of them enjoy playing with modeling clay. There are fun games therapists can play with therapy putty (which is much like modeling clay) to help strengthen the hand and finger muscles to make it easier to use a pen or pencil.

Similarly, working to strengthen core muscles isn't much fun but physical therapists are excellent at developing exciting activities for children or adults to work on these muscles.

Occupational or physical therapists often use creative methods to help patients who are children.

Simple but delicate tasks such as building a tower of toy bricks can help patients regain control of their movements.

Qualify to Be a Therapist

Both occupational and physical therapists need bachelor's degrees with coursework in science. In addition, occupational therapists generally earn a master's degree in occupational therapy and physical therapists must have a Doctor of Physical Therapy (DPT) degree. To practice, both occupational and physical therapists must pass licensing exams.

Therapy Assistant and Aide

If earning a master's in occupational therapy or a DPT to become a physical therapist is not in your future plan but the field sounds interesting, you could think about becoming an assistant or aide to a therapist. Both fields employ therapy assistants and aides, and the educational requirements for these positions are not as demanding as studying to be an occupational therapist or a physical therapist.

Physical therapy assistants and aides work with patients under the supervision of a physical therapist. They don't form treatment plans for the patient but instead they help them with stretching, exercises, and activities to improve their condition as directed by the physical therapist. The same is true for occupational therapy assistants and aides.

Occupational and physical therapy aides typically have a high school diploma and receive their training on the job, whereas occupational and physical therapy assistants are another step up the ladder—they usually have an associate's degree from an accredited therapy program. Being slightly more qualified enables assistants to perform additional duties and more complicated tasks than an aide. Both occupational and physical therapy assistants are required to pass certification exams and earn licenses in most states but aides are not required to become certified or licensed, since they do not do as much hands-on work with patients.

Therapists often use a lot of different equipment to teach patients to become mobile again.

Career Insight:
Going Online

Rob Vining was a physical therapist for many years, working across all settings but Vining decided he was tired of working in a clinic and so took his business into the twenty-first century. He decided to turn his therapy practice into a telehealth practice. Clients who cannot or don't want to come into a clinic can schedule online appointments with Vining's virtual clinic, PTlive. They can chat online with a physical therapist and form a treatment plan. PTlive is even covered by insurance for many patients. Telepractices are common in other medical fields, such as speech therapy and even doctors do teleconsults over the phone but many physiotherapists were unsure that telepractices are beneficial. Vining has proven them wrong and while his practice is thriving, he also co-created a podcast, PT TechTalk, aimed at healthcare professionals who are interested in using technology in patient care.

35

A DAY IN THE LIFE OF
An Occupational Therapist

Occupational therapists can work at medical facilities, schools, therapy clinics, or in homes. The day looks slightly different depending on where the therapist works, but this will give you a peek into a day in the life of an occupational therapist who works in their clients' homes.

8:00 a.m. You're an OT for your state's early intervention program, which means you work with children under the age of three in their homes. Each appointment is an hour but you have to factor in driving time, too, so you leave home bright and early most mornings.

8:30 a.m. You reach the first client's home. Your client is a toddler with autism who has some fine-motor delays. The great thing about working with clients this young is that it's play, play, play! This particular toddler loves art but doesn't have the finger strength to hold crayons or markers, so you're working on that by doing finger painting. You also let him use modeling clay to help strengthen those hand muscles.

9:30 a.m. That was a great way to start your day, and your client is making good progress. You leave to drive to your second client's home, which is quite far away. It's not heavy traffic time, so it'll take you just under half an hour.

10:00 a.m. You arrive at your second client's home. This client is a 16-month-old baby who is working on learning how to pick up finger foods, like pieces of cereal, and self-feed them. Most babies of this age can automatically do this but this baby's disability has left her with minimal strength in her fingers, so she needs a lot of practice. You spend the hour with her working

> You love working with children. They are usually so open to ideas and willing to try new activities.

Some children can be shy or nervous, and you take time to form a relationship with them before introducing too many activities.

on picking up small items for different tasks to keep things fun—sometimes it's cereal to eat, sometimes it's small beads to put in a cup. Anything to encourage that pincer grasp.

11:00 a.m. Your next client is only at 12:00 pm so you have time to get lunch and take a slow drive to reach the client.

12:00 p.m. This is a two-hour appointment because the family has two children receiving therapy from you: a baby and a two-year-old, both with global developmental delays. With the baby, you're working on encouraging him to grasp toys so you use a lot of high-interest toys like rattles and toys with mirrors. With his sister, you're working on sensory issues. She can't stand the feel of anything wet on her, which results in some terrible meltdowns, so you create fun activities that get her used to different sensations and textures, such as finger-painting with shaving cream or creating art with whipped cream.

2:00 p.m. You leave for your fifth client's home. It's a short drive, so you have just enough time to run a quick errand before arriving at the home.

2:30 p.m. Your fifth client is another toddler. He can draw but he doesn't know how to regulate the amount of pressure he puts into his pencil grasp. As a result he ends up breaking pencils and tiring himself out every time he tries to draw or color. That will make writing difficult for him later on, so you do a lot of activities designed to show him the right amount of force to put into fine-motor activities. Watercolors are always a hit, because he can see the picture he's creating without using much pressure at all.

4:00 p.m. You arrive at your last client's house. This client is an almost-three-year-old girl who has low muscle tone as a result of a developmental disability. This means that her body has to work very hard to do simple tasks such as sitting in a chair, and she tires very easily. You spend your sessions trying to build her endurance by doing fun activities like swinging on her tummy, piloting a ride-on vehicle around the house, and playing in a ball pit. It's nothing but fun with this client, even though she has to work so hard!

5:00 p.m. You leave for your drive home, which will take a while because it's rush hour. You're tired because even though your work is all play, it's also a lot of hard work.

Creator
Review and Check In

Now that you've learned about some of the creator roles in science, explore more about how you feel about each job. Use the questions below to help you assess how strongly you feel each role might suit you.

Multimedia Artist and Animator
- Would you enjoy carrying through your creative vision for a project?
- If you work for a large studio, you will need to be a team player. Are you the kind of person who likes to collaborate with others?
- Some artists work as freelancers. Would you like to be your own boss or work for someone else? Why?
- What would you find rewarding about the job? What might the challenges be? How would you deal with those?

Occupational Therapist and Physical Therapist
- Why would you enjoy doing this job?
- Would you be good at thinking creatively to help clients with difficulties? What other skills and personality traits do you have that would make you good at this job?
- What would you find challenging about this job? Would you enjoy meeting these challenges?
- Would you prefer to work in a practice in a team of other therapists or on your own? Why do you say so?

"Ask yourself, 'Will I enjoy doing the job every day?'"

38

"Consider if the career will fit with your values —it's really important."

Therapy Assistant and Aide
- Would you enjoy working under the supervision of a qualified therapist? Why do you say so?
- What do you think you would find challenging about this job? What skills do you have to help you overcome those challenges?

"Think about the financial side of your chosen career—will it suit your lifestyle plans for the future?"

A DAY IN THE LIFE OF An Occupational Therapist

- Review the Day in the Life feature. Did anything about the day surprise you? What was that?
- What do you think the challenges were, and how might you deal with them?
- What aspects of the role do you think you would enjoy?
- Look at the structure of the day and the working hours. Would you be happy with that structure? How might it affect your lifestyle?

Research More

If you like the idea of working as a creator in science, but are not sure the jobs covered in this chapter suit you, here are some more creator roles you could explore.

Science Museum Exhibit Manager
Forensic Reconstruction Artist
Scientific Film Director

CHAPTER FIVE
ORGANIZER ROLES IN SCIENCE

Does turning chaos into order give you a sense of satisfaction? Some people love nothing more than getting things in order: their homework, their bedroom, their summer plans. If you're one of those people, there are a number of science careers that would probably appeal to you. Let's take a look at some.

Technical Writer or Editor

Technical writers and editors are the hidden organizers of the science field, whether that's the medical branch of science or branches such as environmental science, chemistry, or computer science. Whenever any sort of research is done or a breakthrough development made, it has to be documented—for example, the Food and Drug Administration (FDA) requires detailed documentation for every new drug that pharmaceutical companies bring to the market. That information is usually written by a team of scientists and project managers and can consist of thousands of pages of written material. It is then perfected by a team of editors. By the time it gets to the FDA, there can be no mistakes. Similarly, research studies on new treatments for patients have to be documented with extensive writeups, and generally they are published in medical journals, too.

Technical writers must be able to take the details of a complicated scientific project and communicate that data through writing.

Technical writers and editors must organize the text to make scientific documentation understandable for readers, so it must be organized in a logical manner.

Once again, scientists, doctors, and researchers write these articles, and technical editors polish them to make sure they're ready. When new computer software or applications are developed, documentation is involved. It's usually in the form of online help manuals and is written by a technical writer or sometimes the app developer. Either way, it all has to be reviewed by a technical editor.

Good technical documentation starts with the basics and then works its way up to the most difficult pieces. In medical documentation, there's an expected format that must be followed, too. If the FDA received 3,000 pages of random documentation on a new medication, it wouldn't know where to start. All of the information must be carefully organized for the drug to be able to make its way through the process and be approved for patient use.

Technical writers and editors need a bachelor's degree in English, communications, journalism, or a related field. In addition, many employers want technical writers and editors to have some experience with the material they're working with. Some allow on-the-job learning in the particular technology they're writing about or editing but others want people to have some experience in that field. While certifications and licenses are not required for technical writers or editors, there are certain certifications that will open doors for you. For example, the Society for Technical Communication (STC) offers certifications, as does the American Medical Writers Association (AMWA).

Career Insight:
Be Your Own Boss

One great thing about being a technical writer or editor is that you can often be your own boss. There are companies that hire technical writers and editors in-house, meaning in a traditional office-type job with a 40-hour workweek, paid vacations, and health insurance. But more and more, writing and editing jobs are being given to freelance employees who may or may not even come into the office.

Working freelance is a great option for people who like the flexibility of setting their own schedule and working from home (or their favorite coffee shop!). If being able to work in your pajamas or sweats holds appeal, you might want to think about a freelance career. However, it does require you to be disciplined about your work since there's no one around to look over your shoulder and make sure you're doing what you're supposed to be doing. If you tend to procrastinate and are easily distracted, freelance work may not be for you.

Medical Transcriptionist

If medical writing or editing appeals to you but you aren't ready to earn a bachelor's degree, you might consider starting as a medical transcriptionist. Medical transcriptionists listen to dictated voice recordings by healthcare workers and type them into written reports, medical histories, and patient discharge summaries. They are also editors, correcting mistakes made by speech-translation software or errors professionals make when dictating their reports.

To be a medical transcriptionist, you must enjoy working quietly and alone because the job demands that you spend your day listening carefully to recordings.

Being a medical transcriptionist is a great way to find out if working in technical writing is a good fit for you, without having to invest too much time and money into courses. Medical transcriptionists must have a high school diploma and have completed a medical transcription certificate program. These are usually offered at community colleges and vocational schools, though there are some online learning programs, too. As in technical writing and editing, certification is not required but there are opportunities to earn certifications that may open up more job opportunities.

Project Manager

Another way to put your organizational skills to use in the science field is to be a project manager (PM). Many fields use project managers, who do exactly what the roles suggest: They manage projects. They manage the people who work on the project team, they manage the budgets for the project, and they manage the timeline. Organization is vital in this position. PMs have to track every aspect of a project—every dollar that is spent, every hour that is used to work on the project, every piece of paperwork filed, and so on. Being a PM is the ultimate challenge for people who thrive on organization. In many science fields, PMs need to have a bachelor's degree in the field, plus a master's degree in the field or a master's in business administration (MBA). There are also project management certifications that may allow you to take on a management position without a master's degree—it just depends on the company's requirements for advancement.

> Freelance work can be great if you are a self-starter, but if you need someone to organize you, working in a company will probably better suit you.

Pharmaceutical companies employ PMs to make sure that drugs are developed within given time frames and to set budgets.

Career Insight:
Project Management Pay

The Project Management Institute (PMI) recently compiled salary information from US PMs who hold a project management professional (PMP) certification, and determined the top five highest-paying PM positions. Engineering PMs came in at number five on the list. They came from huge software engineering companies such as Google, Microsoft, and Apple. Number four on the list was aerospace PMs, who work for companies such as Boeing, Airbus, and Lockheed Marin to make sure that new aircraft are built and delivered on time and within the approved budget. Number three on the list was pharmaceutical PMs who work on prescription drug development, ensuring that they stay on schedule and within their budget. Number two was consulting PMs, who work for consulting companies. Consulting companies work with other companies in various industries to help them bring projects to successful completion. And finally, the top paying job for PMs was in resources. These managers work in industries that grow and extract natural resources, such as coal and oil, and agriculture.

Medical and Health Services Manager

Medical and health services managers are also called healthcare administrators. They work in a variety of different healthcare facilities, such as hospitals, medical practices, and rehabilitation centers. In some cases, they manage a specific department of a hospital or medical office but in others, those who are very experienced may manage the entire hospital or healthcare facility.

It's the manager's job to ensure that the department or facility runs as efficiently as possible and that the quality of patient care is high. They also make sure that the facility is complying with all laws and regulations—in healthcare, there are many. Failure to comply with laws and regulations could mean hefty fines or even closure. Administrators also create work schedules for facility employees and manage the facility's budget. They also keep detailed records of all of the facility's services and a record of the budget.

When there is a public event, such as the opening of a new wing of a hospital or a board meeting, the healthcare administrator is usually the person who attends on behalf of the department or facility. Healthcare administrators who are in charge of a specific department at a larger facility act as the contact between staff members and facility administration.

Healthcare administrators must have at least a bachelor's degree, and many have master's degrees. The degrees can be in health administration, health management, nursing, public health administration, business administration, or a related field. Most employers also want healthcare administrators to have experience working in the field—whether as a lower-level administrator or in a clinical role, such as nursing.

Healthcare administrators regularly meet with department heads to make sure schedules and budgets are met.

45

A DAY IN THE LIFE OF
A Technical Editor

Technical editors sometimes work in an office but often they work at home and contract to multiple clients. This day-in-the-life will give you an insight into what a freelance technical editor does.

8:00 a.m. Today you are working from home, so you can take your time getting up and ready. To start with, you check your emails to see what, if anything, you need to address. There's always something that needs to be answered, and today is no exception. You spend the next 30 minutes answering questions from a few clients while you eat your breakfast.

8:30 a.m. You're quite an organized person and like to jot down a rough schedule for your day. You do this every morning because being a freelancer and working for multiple clients can be a bit of a juggling act. Sometimes, your days are rammed but other days, you have time to spare—it just depends on how things work out.

9:00 a.m. You begin working on a technical report for a major manufacturer. There are a lot of difficult computations and explanations in the report, so it requires a lot of focus. That's why you schedule yourself to work on that report first, when your mind is still fresh.

> You love the fact that you can change your work environment whenever you like. That's one of the great things about being freelance.

Technical editing can be very intense. Sometimes, you have to take a break and revisit your work later when your brain is rested.

12:00 p.m. Your mind feels muddled from three hours of difficult technical work so you decide to take a break to go to the gym. That's the beauty of working from home—you can pick and choose your work hours, as long as you get your projects done on time.

2:00 p.m. You arrive home after a good workout and a lunch break to get straight back to the technical report for one more hour. That's not long enough to finish it but you still have several days left before the deadline, so you can pick it up tomorrow.

3:00 p.m. You change to a less difficult report. This is an audit for a government agency. It's still considered technical work but it's not nearly as difficult as the manufacturing report, so you can do it later in the day, when your brain is a little more tired. Sometimes, you like to do this work in a coffee shop, just for a change of scenery—and a fresh cup of coffee!

5:00 p.m. You stop editing for the day. Although your projects aren't complete, you know that five to six hours is the longest an editor can do good work in a day. You save the less brain-intensive work for the end of the day, when you're tired. It's time to send out invoices to a few clients and do a little work on your business website. Both tasks need to be done but they don't require the intense concentration of editing, so you save them for later in the day.

7:30 p.m. You sign off for the night, knowing that tomorrow is going to be another busy day.

Organizer
Review and Check In

Now that you've learned about some of the organizer roles in science, explore more about how you feel about each job. Use the questions below to help you assess how strongly you feel each role might suit you.

Technical Writer or Editor
- These jobs require research to keep up to date with the latest technology. Is this something you would enjoy? Why do you say so?
- Are you able to follow a brief and take instructions from clients? What skills do you have that would make you good at this? What would you find challenging about this type of work?

Medical Transcriptionist
- Would you be happy to study further toward being a certified transcriptionist?
- Why would you enjoy this job?
- To do this job, you would need excellent listening and typing skills. Would this be a challenge for you? How could you improve on these skills to ensure you are good at your job?

"Always keep an eye on the future and how your career might change. For example, will technological advancements change some aspects of your job?"

"Think about what makes you unique. How could you use that to your advantage in a career?"

Project Manager
- Would you be happy to manage a large team of people and make sure they are completing their jobs well and on time?
- How do you think being a PM might suit your personality? Why do you say so?

Medical and Health Services Manager
- What do you find interesting about this role?
- Would you be happy to manage a large team and make sure they are doing their jobs well and on time? How would you deal with those who are not?

"Never rush into career decisions. Always take your time, and work through all your options."

Research More

If you like the idea of working as an organizer in science, but are not sure the jobs covered in this chapter suit you, here are some more organizer roles you could explore.

Science Museum Curator
Science Museum Exhibit Coordinator
Archivist

CHAPTER SIX

THINKER ROLES IN SCIENCE

Thinkers generally like to take their time making decisions, and analyze all the available information before they do so. They like to imagine every possible scenario and every possible outcome. There are many possible careers for thinkers in science—especially in the field of research.

Medical Scientist

If medicine and human health are your passions, and research is one of your talents and something you enjoy, you might want to think about becoming a medical scientist. Medical scientists investigate diseases as well as treatments designed to improve human health. They also work on clinical trials to try to bring those treatments to reality.

Often their research consists of forming hypotheses about topics such as how diseases spread, how cells mutate, and how treatments can fight disease and improve human health. They then need to create experiments to test these hypotheses. If their theory works in the first experiments, they'll go on to develop more experiments to continue testing. Eventually, that

> Medical scientists love research. Many of their projects take months if not years to complete, so being dedicated to the job is essential.

> Human beings are fascinating! If you become a sociologist, you will be able to study human behavior.

may lead to the clinical trial stage for promising treatments. If a treatment involves prescription drugs, medical scientists also help standardize the drug's dosage and potency, so that the drug can eventually be mass-produced for patient use.

Becoming a medical scientist requires a lot of schooling. Most medical scientists have a bachelor's degree in biology, chemistry, or a related field. They then usually earn a PhD in a life science, such as biology, although some choose to get a medical degree instead of or in addition to the PhD. Either way, it demands a great deal of training and a test of perseverance and determination. There's no particular certification required to be a medical scientist but any medical scientist who is involved in treating patients or administering drugs must be licensed to practice as a physician.

Sociologist

A science field you might not have thought of that is an excellent one for thinkers is sociology. Sociologists study social behavior by carefully observing groups, cultures, and social institutions. They set up and conduct surveys, observe individuals and social groups of people, and conduct interviews. Then they analyze the data they've collected to make conclusions. They generally prepare reports or presentations to share their findings. Often, their findings are about the potential impact of some type of social change or the problems in a particular part of society. For example, sociologists may study crime in areas of high poverty, or the poor health outcomes for African American mothers and babies.

Sociologists must complete a bachelor's degree, which includes coursework in sociology, social statistics, research methods, and social theory. To find work in the field, usually sociologists complete a master's degree or a PhD. There are also options to be certified.

Gathering criminal evidence is painstaking work. Each piece of evidence must be identified and its position at the crime scene marked.

Forensic Science Technician

Criminology is a very interesting branch of sociology. It focuses on crime and society. If crime and investigation interests you, you might consider a career as a forensic science technician. You would work with police departments and other law enforcement officials to collect and analyze crime scene evidence that the investigating officers can then use to help them solve crimes.

To help solve cases, forensic science technicians may take photographs of crime scenes, make meticulous notes about the position of evidence found at the scene, and catalog any evidence collected so that it can be transported to the crime lab and eventually stored. Sometimes, they also help reconstruct crime scenes to figure out the sequence of events and how the crime happened.

Back at the lab, forensic science technicians perform analysis on the collected crime scene evidence. This may involve looking for fingerprints and then matching those to suspects and collecting deoxyribonucleic acid (DNA) and running it through various databases to check for a match. This is complex work and forensic science technicians must be meticulous and pay careful attention to detail. Handling evidence is an incredibly delicate procedure, because any mishandling could potentially produce incorrect results and jeopardize the police force's case.

Most forensic science technicians have a bachelor's degree in forensic science, biology, chemistry, or a related field. Many also earn a master's degree in forensic science or a related field. As with many careers, a higher qualification will usually offer more job opportunities. If you are interested in working specifically with a police department, you can train at the police academy first and then, once you are qualified, you can train as a crime scene investigator. If you choose this route, you don't necessarily need a bachelor's degree. On-the-job training is required for forensic science technicians, whether they work at crime scenes or in the lab.

Forensic scientists carefully examine items from a crime scene to look for evidence such as blood stains and hairs.

Career Insight:
Forensic Science Options

Forensic science is a broad field and has a lot of specialized careers under its umbrella. For example, arson investigators are forensic scientists who use their extensive knowledge of chemistry and fire behavior to investigate cases of arson. Arson is when someone deliberately sets fire to something. Computer forensics examiners use their knowledge of data retrieval to recover information from computers that may implicate a suspect in a crime. Forensic anthropologists examine human remains to determine the cause of death and the person's identity (if it's not already known). Similarly, forensic pathologists and medical examiners perform autopsies to try to determine a person's cause of death. Finally, forensic toxicologists perform tests on body tissue and fluid samples to determine the presence of drugs or other chemical substances in a person's body.

Agricultural and Food Science Technician

If you love research but you aren't sure whether pursuing a master's degree or PhD is in your future, investigate becoming a technician. Some scientific fields use technicians to do the measuring and analysis work that requires a lot of attention to detail. One example is agricultural and food science technicians. They collect and analyze food samples (vegetable, fruit, and animal) to ensure that the quality is of the correct standard and that the food is safe for human consumption. They also analyze the equipment used to produce the food, the ingredients fed to animals that are going to be consumed as food, and test the additives that are put into food to preserve it. They keep detailed records of their findings and alert the authorities if there's any suspected contamination of a food.

Most agricultural and food science technicians have at least an associate's degree in biology, chemistry, animal science, crop science, or a related field. Some have bachelor's degrees and others have only a high school degree but have related work experience in the field or on-the-job training.

Sustainable food production will be one of the most important areas of research in the future as we try to find ways to feed Earth's growing population without harming the planet.

Career Insight:
No Degree Needed

Many of the science careers for thinkers require a college degree—at the very least, an associate's degree or even advanced degrees. However, there is an excellent job for thinkers that doesn't necessarily require a college degree: coding.

Coders, or computer programmers, write and test code that produces applications and software. The field is wide open, since new applications are being developed all the time. A degree in computer science will get you far in this field but it's also not a hard-and-fast requirement to being a successful coder. Some application and software developers are willing to overlook the lack of a college degree if a promising coder with great talent applies for a job.

Coding can be self-taught to a certain extent. There are books and many websites that will teach you the basics of coding in many languages. You can also just sit down with a free integrated development environment and start testing out your coding skills. Coding is very much a learn-by-doing skill and there are many online tutorials that can help you get started.

There are many programming languages out there but you can start by learning a good general-purpose one, such as Java or Python. Once you've learned one language, it's fairly easy to learn new ones. Although the syntax is different in each, they generally follow the same patterns for development. If you want to get a high-level software development job at some point in the future, you'll probably want to work toward a degree. But to start out in the coding world, you don't necessarily need one if you can demonstrate that you have the skills an employer is looking for.

A DAY IN THE LIFE OF A Forensic Science Technician

Many forensic science technicians work either in the lab or out in the field. Here, we'll look at a day in the life of a forensic scientist who has a chance to do both.

8:00 a.m. You arrive at the lab, ready for a day of testing blood and DNA samples. You check with your colleagues to see what's new—whether any high-priority requests for processing have come in. Nothing has, so you set to work on the samples that were delivered yesterday from a crime scene. It was at an apartment complex, so there was a lot of evidence collected—some of which may have nothing to do with the crime but all of which needs to be tested to rule out any connection.

9:30 a.m. You're told that you're needed out in the field. This is an unusual request—you usually spend your days in the lab but the local police force is short of a couple of field forensic scientists, and they need someone to fill in. You did fieldwork for a while before switching to the lab, so you're a good candidate.

10:00 a.m. You arrive at the crime scene. A mini-mart was robbed and a witness says that the robber threw his weapon in the dumpster. You aren't sure what other evidence he might have thrown in there, so you need to go through all the trash in the dumpster and bag-and-tag anything that you think might possibly relate to the crime. It's hard to rule anything out so you're going to be bagging and tagging for a while. It's hot and smelly work but if you can find useful evidence, it'll be worth it.

Checking for fingerprints is a basic but important part of your job. It can help reveal who was at a crime scene.

12:00 p.m. It's time to break for lunch. Eating is the last thing you want to do when you've been sorting through trash for three hours but you're getting fatigued and know you need to eat something and drink some more water.

12:30 p.m. You spend the next two hours sorting through the rest of the garbage and, when everything is tagged, you ask the other investigators on the scene what they need next. They're pretty well caught up, but then someone calls in a tip that the robber may have thrown a piece of clothing over a nearby fence, so you have to go over to that yard and search for the item. You find it so photograph it and log its location in case the investigators need it, then carefully bag and tag the evidence and arrange for it to be sent back to the lab.

2:30 p.m. You're back at the lab—and now running behind on your day's work, because you were called to the field so you waste no time in collecting DNA from the evidence collected at the apartment complex and sending it off for analysis.

5:00 p.m. You finally finish with the apartment evidence and go check your emails. Some DNA reports have come back from another crime, so you need to run them through the law enforcement database to see whether any are a match to known criminals.

> You know that the smallest objects, such as used cigarettes, can reveal vital evidence, including the DNA of the smoker.

It could wait for tomorrow but you don't like the idea of leaving crimes unsolved any longer than you have to, so you go ahead and run them through the computer systems to find out more.

6:30 p.m. As it turns out, one is a match for a man on parole in a neighboring county. You put in a call to the investigators on that case and let them know of the match so they can arrest the man. Your day's work is done and you feel like you've made a big difference.

Thinker
Review and Check In

Now that you've learned about some of the thinker roles in science, explore more about how you feel about each job. Use the questions below to help you assess how strongly you feel each role might suit you.

Medical Scientist
- What is it about this work that you would find satisfying?
- Would you be happy to undertake the training involved for this job?
- This job may involve spending a lot of time working on one project. Would you enjoy this?
- What would you find rewarding about the job? What might the challenges be?

Sociologist
- What skills do you have that would suit this job?
- This job involves setting up and conducting surveys. Is this something you would enjoy? Why?
- To do this job, you need excellent communication skills. If this is not your strength, how can you improve?

"Close your eyes and picture yourself doing your ideal job in the future. What type of workplace setting are you in and what are you doing? Keep that vision in mind as you research careers."

"Write down your top five strengths and weaknesses on a piece of paper. Keep it to hand and use it to work through career options."

Forensic Science Technician
- You could be called to work at any time of the day or night. How would this impact your lifestyle?
- What skills would you need to do this job?

Agricultural and Food Science Technician
- How would you feel about working with others to complete a project?
- What about this job appeals to you?
- What would you find challenging about doing this job?

"Once you know what career you'd like to follow, make a flowchart that shows all the steps you need to take to get to that career—then follow it!"

Research More

If you like the idea of working as a thinker in science, but are not sure the jobs covered in this chapter suit you, here are some more thinker roles you could explore.

Geoscientist
Hydrologist
Microbiologist

WHAT NEXT?—YOUR CAREER CHECKLIST

If you have come to the end of this book and are ready to start making a career in science a reality, follow the checklist on these pages to kick-start your future.

Start at School

For any science-based career, you will of course need exceptional science skills, so pay attention in your science class. For all science roles, you should also work on your English skills, because you will need to be able to communicate your scientific findings effectively.

If your school offers consumer science courses with nursing as options, and you think you may like to pursue a career in nursing or as an orderly, make sure you sign up for them.

Creator roles in science will allow you to mix your creative talents with your interest in science. Choose subjects at school that will help you develop this career area. For example, studying visual arts at school will help you carve out a career in scientific art and animation. Also explore course options that offer computer-aided design and drafting (CADD).

Organizer roles in science such as technical writer or editor and transcriptionist will require both a great grasp of science and good command of English, so make sure you focus on both classes at school. If you move into project management, you will need to be able to use information technology (IT) efficiently, so if your school offers an IT course as an option, make sure you sign up for it. In it, you'll become familiar with many different skills you'll likely need in an organizer role, such as learning to use word-processing software and spreadsheets. You will also need good math skills in any management roles, so give your math class full attention.

Talk to a Guidance Counselor

If your guidance counselor offers career advice, take it! Guidance counselors will be able to help you explore a lot of different options and talk more about whether a role in science could suit you. They will also be able to advise you on further education courses you could pursue after school or in-job training that could suit you.

60

 **Get Connected**

Your parents and parents' friends may have great contacts in the science world. They may be able to put you in touch with an employer, so that you can talk to them directly about roles in science that interest you. For example, a parent or friend could connect you with an alternative energy company, so that you can talk to the people who work there about the roles they carry out.

 **Get Experience**

The best way to find out if a career is really going to suit you is to try it out! However, because roles in science naturally require a significant amount of training before a person can start working in the field, you will not be able to get real work experience until you start your training in your chosen area. At that point, you may be able to get an internship position, which is an unpaid temporary role in which people can get work experience. Internships provide real-world experience, which is invaluable to science students.

 **Walk in Their Shoes**

Some employers are happy to have students meet with them in person for informational interviews, through which you can find out what people in science roles do. You may even be able to shadow someone who works in science. For example, you could spend a day or two at work with an environmental engineer, finding out more about what they do and how they do it. That's a really great way to discover if you would like to do their job in the future.

 **Do Your Research**

You can never do enough research when it comes to planning a future career, so explore as many resources as you can to find out more. Start by taking a look at the resources on page 63 of this book to learn more. For example, the U.S. Bureau of Labor Statistics (BLS) offers some great resources that can help you learn more about possible roles in science. Check out in particular their Occupational Outlook Handbook section.

As you research, remember there is never a right or wrong in making choices, and you can always change your mind. Keep flexible, be positive about your future, and have fun choosing your perfect STEM career.

GLOSSARY

analysis detailed examination of something, usually for the purpose of drawing conclusions

associate's degree a two-year degree awarded by a community college

biodiesel a biofuel that replaces standard diesel fuel

bioenergy renewable energy produced by living organisms

biofuel a fuel created from living matter

core muscles the muscles in the torso, which make up the core of the body's strength

deoxyribonucleic acid (DNA) the carrier of each living organism's genetic code

developmental delay a condition in which a person's development is slower than what is usually expected for the person's age

freelance working for multiple companies or people as a self-employed individual, rather than being employed by just one organization

genetic related to inherited characteristics

integrated development environment an application that provides a place in which developers can build and test new software

life sciences the study of living organisms

pacemaker an artificial device implanted in the heart that stimulates heart muscle to regulate heartbeat

pharmaceutical related to medicinal drugs

PhD doctor of philosophy degree. PhD degrees are available in many subjects

photovoltaic describes production of electrical current when a substance is exposed to light

physical therapy a type of therapy and exercise that promotes movement and mobility

prosthetist a person who creates artificial body parts, such as limbs or certain organs

rehabilitation centers medical facilities where patients stay while they work on regaining their health or mobility after injury or illness

renewable a source of power that is not depleted by use

samples small sections of tissue

software the programs and operating system used by a computer

sustainable able to be maintained without causing damage to the environment

syntax a set of rules that determines the arrangement of terms to create a usable language

telehealth healthcare provided by telecommunications technology

traumatized deeply upset by an experience

turbines power-producing machines in which a rotor is fitted with fans that turn as air flows through them

vocational school a school that is designed to teach the skills necessary for certain occupations

FIND OUT MORE

Books
Lewis, Daniel. *Computers, Communication & the Arts* (Careers in Demand for High School Graduates). Mason Crest Publishers, 2018.

Mooney, Carla. *Careers in Computer Science* (Exploring Careers). Referencepoint Press, 2017.

Oxlade, Chris. *Dream Jobs in Science* (Cutting-Edge Careers in STEM). Crabtree Publishing Company, 2017.

Raines, Noreen. *Nerdy Jobs in STEM: 21 Careers in Science, Technology, Engineering, and Math That Make It Cool to Be Smart*. CreateSpace Independent Publishing, 2017.

Websites
Take a look at the BLS site for more careers guidance:
www.bls.gov/k12/students/careers/how-can-bls-help-me-explore-careers.htm

Check out the BLS Occupational Outlook Handbook to find out more about different jobs and the qualifications you need for them:
www.bls.gov/ooh

If you're interested in the cutting-edge science of artificial intelligence (AI), check out this interactive site that allows you to play with and create AI:
www.curiositymachine.org

This site is a fun repository of anything and everything science-related. If you want to know how something works, you'll find the answer here:
https://science.howstuffworks.com

This website connects teens with experiential learning opportunities, including summer programs, community service opportunities, and other programs:
www.teenlife.com

Publisher's note to educators and parents:
All the websites featured above have been carefully reviewed to ensure that they are suitable for students. However, many websites change often, and we cannot guarantee that a site's future contents will continue to meet our high standards of educational value. Please be advised that students should be closely monitored whenever they access the Internet.

INDEX

agricultural and food science technicians 54, 59
Airbus 44
alternative energy installers and technicians 24, 29
American Medical Writers Association (AMWA)
Apple 44
biomedical engineers 22, 28
Boeing 44
budgets 43, 44, 45
builder personality and roles 5, 6, 8, 20–21, 22, 23, 24, 25, 26, 27
certification 21, 25, 35, 43, 44, 48, 51
coding 55
college 10, 14, 55
community college 12, 24, 43
competency exams 12
considering challenges of the job 18, 19, 28, 29, 38, 39, 48, 58, 59
considering rewards of the job 18, 28, 38, 48, 49, 58
considering working as part of a team 18, 19, 38, 49, 59
considering your finances 39
considering your lifestyle 18, 29, 39, 59
considering your skills 18, 19, 28, 29, 38, 39, 48, 58, 59
considering your values 29
considering your work environment 4, 29, 46
consumer science courses at school 60
creator personality and roles 5, 30–31, 32, 33, 34, 35, 36, 37, 38, 39
degrees 10, 11, 12, 14, 21, 22, 23, 25, 31, 34, 35, 41, 42, 43, 45, 51, 52, 54, 55
diplomas 11, 12, 15, 21, 24, 35, 43
doctors 10, 18, 41, 51
English classes at school 60
environmental engineers 22, 23, 25, 29, 61
exploring options 9, 55
flowcharts 5, 6–7, 8, 59
forensic animators 32
forensic science technicians 52, 53, 56–57, 59

GED 21
genetic engineers 23
Google 44
guidance counselors 60, 61
helper personality and roles 5, 6, 10–11, 12, 13, 14, 15, 16, 17, 18, 19
high school 15, 21, 24, 25, 35, 43
information technology (IT) courses at school 60
informational interviews 61
internships 61
IT courses at school 60
licenses 11, 14, 21, 34, 35, 41, 51
making connections 61
math classes at school 60
medical and health services managers 45, 49
medical appliance technicians 21, 28
medical assistants 10, 16
medical school 10, 11
medical scientists 50, 58
medical transcriptionists 42, 43, 48, 60
Microsoft 44
multimedia artists and animators 30, 31, 38
nurses 10, 11, 12, 13, 16–17, 18, 45, 60
nursing assistants 12, 18
nursing outside of hospitals 13
occupational therapists and physical therapists 32, 33, 34, 36–37, 38, 39
on-the-job training 21, 25, 41, 53, 54, 60
online learning and tuition 43, 55
orderlies 12, 19, 60

Pixar 30
portfolios 31
project managers (PMs) 43, 44, 49, 60
prosthetists and orthotists 20, 21, 26–27, 28
radiologists 10
research 8, 9, 19, 29, 39, 49, 59, 61
researchers 10
resumes 61
robotics 22
salaries 11, 44
schedules 44, 45
science classes at school 14, 60
self-employment 38, 42, 43, 46–47
Society for Technical Communication (STC) 41
sociologists 51, 58
switching careers 9
technical school 25
technical writers and editors 40, 41, 46–47, 48, 60
the environment 22, 23, 24, 25, 54, 61
therapy assistants and aides 34, 39
vet school 14, 19
veterinarians 10, 14, 15, 19
veterinary technicians and assistants 10, 14, 15, 19
visual arts at school 60
vocational school 12, 24, 43
wildlife biologists 15
working from home 42, 47
working hours 16–17, 26–27, 29, 36–37, 39, 42, 46–47, 49, 56–57

About the Author

Cathleen Small has written many books for young people on a wide variety of topics. In writing this book she has learned the value of personality testing, research, and considering many options when exploring a future career.